KRISTEN JACKS
Founder of Money in Your Twenties^{SM}

INVESTING

Your lively, jargon-free guide to getting started

DK

ISBN: 979-8-218-34059-9

To my beloved daughters

Special thanks to:

Sally Bednar

Susan Kitchens Kwun

Kris Tonski

Disclaimer

This book is for educational and informational purposes only. It is not intended to provide financial, legal, tax or investment advice.

Information offered in this book is provided "as is" without any express or implied warranty of any kind, including warranties of fitness for a particular purpose. In no event shall the author, Kristen Jacks, and/or DK Advisors, LLC (d/b/a Money in Your Twenties℠) be liable to any party for any damages of any kind, including but not limited to direct, indirect, special or consequential damages for any use of this book including, without limitation, lost profits, tax liability or loss of income.

If you need financial, legal, tax or investment advice, before you make any financial decisions, the author urges you to consult a qualified financial advisor, insurance agent, tax attorney, enrolled agent or other qualified professional who is fully aware of your individual circumstances. The author does not warrant or guarantee the correctness, completeness, accuracy, timeliness or fitness of any information or products or services mentioned in this book.

Contents

Introduction

Brooke scans the glossy brochure from her new employer. Beneath a long, green arrow containing the word "conservative" on one end and "aggressive" on the other, the brochure lists 20 investment options. There's the "Fidelity Mid Cap Index Fund," the "PIMCO Total Return Fund," and the "JP Morgan Small Cap Value Fund," among others.

Brooke feels lucky to have an employer that offers a 401(k), but the investments that go in it are confusing. Does the "Fidelity Government Money Market Fund" have something to do with getting money from the government? Maybe the "Fidelity Real Estate Index Fund" will help her to save for a house?

Unable to decode the baffling options, Brooke decides to put her money in the "Invesco High Yield Fund." She likes the sound of high yield (it's what she looked for when she opened a bank account), and the fund is listed as a conservative bond fund. She has always heard that bonds are safe.

Poor Brooke. Over the next five years, the Invesco High Yield Fund would average only a 4% return. The fund was also misplaced under the "conservative" investments in the brochure. "High Yield" bonds go by another name – junk bonds. Brooke assumed unnecessary risk with no reward.

Unprepared

Most young adults are unprepared to navigate the complex world of investing. As Jim Cramer lamented on his investing TV show, *Mad Money*, "The only thing they almost never teach you in high school, let alone touch with a 10-foot pole in college, is financial literacy. Money is just not talked about in education."

Research confirms the dearth of financial education in America. According to one large study by Champlain College, almost half of all states in the U.S. earned a letter grade of "C," "D" or "F" when it comes to offering financial literacy classes in high school.

My home state of Connecticut received an "F," as did California, the largest state in the union. Washington, D.C., home of the legislators who could fix this problem, also got an "F."

Inaccessible

When the poet Samuel Taylor Coleridge wrote "Water, water everywhere, nor any drop to drink," he was describing sailors surrounded by salt water who could not quench their thirst.

Similarly, you are surrounded by finance books and financial media, but your basic needs go unmet. The problem is that books, podcasts, magazines, and newspapers are too sophisticated. They assume a level of knowledge you probably never attained.

Best-selling books like *The Intelligent Investor* and *A Random Walk Down Wall Street* are only useful if you already understand the stock market. Bloomberg podcasters speak as though you majored in Economics in college. *The Wall Street Journal* ignores the novice investor.

Inaccurate

Worse than inaccessible discourse is inaccurate "guidance." The influencer community is great for skin care products and music recommendations, but shockingly uninformed about stocks and bonds.

One popular investing podcaster made this claim: "…if you wanna buy an individual bond, you gotta come with cash. You can't just buy one for like 30 bucks, you gotta buy tens of thousands, if not hundreds of thousands, of dollars worth of bonds. You cannot buy them through Fidelity brokerage account, you have to go to a separate entity to try to buy the bonds. It's not easy to do as an individual investor."

This statement is COMPLETELY FALSE.

Many high-quality bonds are sold in increments of $1,000, and they are easily purchased through Fidelity or Schwab or another online broker.

If $1,000 is too costly, visit treasurydirect.gov to buy I bonds. They are backed by the full faith and credit of the United States government, and the minimum purchase is $25.

Your Guide

In these pages, you will find the basic guide you need to begin your investing journey. The goal of this book is to make sure no young adult is left behind. Here is the solid foundation you did not receive at home or school.

Clear headings, jargon-free language, and brief descriptions are the norm for this book. You will also find familiar companies and interesting stories that make investing accessible and relatable.

This book has been painstakingly researched. Sources and references can be found in the **Notes section**. If you have questions about any of the facts in this book, email questions@moneyinyourtwenties.com and your inquiry will be handled promptly.

Not a beginner?

This book serves anyone who has gaps in learning. Investors who understand stocks may need help with bonds. If you are investing outside of your 401(k), then you need to learn the serious tax consequences of investing.

Too often personal finance is tedious and boring. This book isn't. You might even enjoy reading this.

Shall we begin?

Chapter 1

The Language of Investing

In his book, *How to Speak Money*, John Lanchester wonders if financial professionals confuse us with jargon to control us or if, as he puts it, "The language of money is complicated because the underlying realities are complicated."

It does seem odd that words used in investing don't match their everyday meaning. Who would guess that "coupon" is the interest paid on a bond?

One thing is clear. You cannot easily decode financial language. To address this problem, Lanchester created a dictionary to demystify investment terms.

If your goal is to develop a broad and deep understanding of finance and economics, then keep Lanchester's lexicon handy. If your aim is to learn enough to review 401(k) options or buy your first stock, then this chapter is for you.

One word to rule them all

The abbreviation "cap" is only three letters but it's a mighty term in investing. Cap stands for "market capitalization" which refers to the dollar value of a company based on its stock price.

Recall "cap" was embedded in the baffling investment options in the first chapter ("Fidelity Mid **Cap** Index Fund" and "JP Morgan Small **Cap** Value Fund").

Consider these examples.

Company	Market Capitalization
Apple	$3 Trillion
Amazon	$1.5 Trillion
Visa	$517 Billion
Disney	$172 Billion
Allstate	$36 Billion
Williams Sonoma	$12 Billion
H&R Block	$7 Billion

Shake Shack	$3 Billion
Six Flags	$2 Billion
Petco	$992 million
Biolife Solutions	$557 million
Build-A-Bear	$376 million
Rent the Runway	$40 million

Source: Yahoo! Finance, 11/28/2023

Market capitalization is calculated by multiplying the company's current stock price by the total number of shares outstanding.

Don't worry. You don't have to do the math. Financial apps like Yahoo! Finance typically list a company's market cap along with other data points like the company's highest and lowest stock price in the past year.

Relative Size

It is important to know what market cap is because professional money managers use it to segment the universe of investable stocks. They divide stocks into "small," "mid," and "large" size companies based on market cap.

9

Thus, the "Fidelity Mid Cap Index Fund" is focused on companies with mid-range market capitalizations like H&R Block.

The "JP Morgan Small Cap Value Fund" invests in companies with relatively small market caps like Petco.

Large Cap funds invest in stocks with relatively large market caps like Amazon, Disney, and Visa.

Growth versus Value

Another way money managers segment the stock market is by growth versus value.

Growth companies are ones that are growing quickly. For example, ETSY tripled sales revenue from 2019 to 2022.

	2022	2021	2020	2019
ETSY Revenue:	$2,566,111	$2,329,114	$1,725,625	$818,379

Any company that is rapidly increasing its customers or market share or profits will likely fall in the growth category.

The concept of "value" is more complicated. The "value" label often falls on established companies that are not growing rapidly (think Walmart or Exxon).

We will talk more about value in the chapters devoted to stocks.

Invisible Giants

Everyone knows big companies like Apple, Disney, and Coca-Cola; few young adults can name the largest asset managers like Fidelity or Vanguard. These companies are invisible giants.

They are also the first thing you see when you read 401(k) investment options.

Now you can decode these options yourself. The "Fidelity Mid Cap Index Fund" is an investment run by one of the invisible giants – Fidelity – that invests in companies with a mid-range market capitalization.

That wasn't so hard, right?

Last words

"Every industry has its own vocabulary," says Pulitzer prize-winning author Gary Rivlin. "The shorthand and jargon can sound like gibberish to an outsider, but they form a code that offers entry into that world."

As you enter the world of investing, resist the urge to infer meaning when you see investing jargon. Use Google and learn something new.

Chapter 2

What Is a Stock?

Which of these two scenarios best describes you?

Scenario A: The Hoka running shoe is a hot new trend. Everyone is buying them. You buy a pair, too.

Scenario B: The Hoka running shoe is a hot new trend. Everyone is buying them. You buy shares in the company that makes Hokas.

If scenario B sounds implausible, then you probably did not grow up in a family that discussed stocks.

This chapter aims to educate you about what stocks are and why they exist.

Where Companies Get Money to Grow

If you had to guess where a small business goes to get money to expand, "the bank" is a good answer. Banks do make loans to all sorts of small businesses like beauty salons, contractors, co-working spaces, restaurants, and gyms.

However, some businesses have access to more sophisticated financing options. These are companies with visionary leaders and massive growth potential.

Referred to as "start-ups," these companies draw interest from private investors and venture capital (VC) firms. The most successful start-ups have the option to raise money by issuing stock to the public through an initial public offering (IPO).

Take Starbucks for example.

Starbucks

Before 1990, there were fewer than 100 Starbucks in the entire world. Yes. You read that correctly. What most of us have experienced at Starbucks - the pairing of exceptional coffee with a sense of community – was only an idea in the early 1980s. This idea slowly gained momentum, but popularity alone does not build new stores. Money does.

Starbucks was a classic start-up. It had a visionary leader -

Howard Schultz – and massive growth potential.

Initially, Schultz expanded his company by raising money from private investors. In his book, *Pour Your Heart Into It*, Schultz describes a grueling year in 1986 where he approached 242 potential investors and got 217 rejections. He raised $1.65 million, but the process was exhausting.

By 1990, Schultz was able to convince venture capital firms to help fund Starbucks's growth. Initially, VC firms kicked in $13.5 million. They added another $15 million the following year.

What did all this money do for Starbucks? In four years, Starbucks opened 99 stores and turned a profit.

By 1992, Starbucks had enough of a track record of success to do an initial public offering (IPO). IPOs are fundraising on steroids.

In an IPO, shares of stock in a private company are made available for the public to purchase. If the IPO is handled correctly by the investment bankers who manage it, the IPO can produce a windfall for the company to use to continue to grow.

On June 26, 1992, the Starbucks IPO raised $29 million in one day. While that may sound like a modest sum, it was a lot of money back then, and fueled Starbucks's growth.

By 1996 Starbucks had 1,000 stores and continued to grow exponentially.

Netflix

Not all start-ups endure significant rejection while trying to raise money. If a start-up is run by a leader with a proven track record, venture capital money is easier to tap.

In his book *That Will Never Work,* Netflix co-founder Marc Randolph dubbed his partner, Reed Hastings, "venture capitalist catnip." Randolph credits Netflix's relatively smooth VC fundraising with the fact that Hastings had a reputation for being a business "miracle worker."

Netflix was launched in 1998, raised $100 million among VCs, and had its IPO on May 23, 2002. The IPO raised $82.5 million by issuing 5.5 million shares at a price of $15 per share.

Instacart

Buyer demand, the impact of inflation, and favorable market conditions have dramatically increased the amount of money companies can raise in an IPO.

On September 19, 2023, the grocery delivery company Instacart raised $660 million by issuing 22 million shares of stock at a price of $30.

Definition

Starbucks, Netflix, and Instacart all raised money by issuing stock to the public. But what is a stock?

Barron's *Dictionary of Finance and Investment Terms* defines stock as ownership of a corporation represented by shares that are a claim on the corporation's earnings and assets.

Stocks are also referred to as equities.

They are a sub-group of "securities," a broad financial term used to describe a wide range of investments, including stocks and bonds.

When you purchase a stock, you own a tiny fraction of the company that issued the stock.

Ticker Symbols

Ted, Sue, and Ben have one thing in common: a name shortened for simplicity. Publicly traded companies are the same. They have a short name – a ticker symbol – to identify them.

For example, the ticker symbol for Starbucks is SBUX and the ticker for Netflix is NFLX. Instacart's ticker is CART.

For some companies with short names, their name is their ticker (e.g., UBER and ETSY).

Some companies have fun ticker symbols that relate to their products or customers. For example:

TAP for Molson Coors

MTN for Vail Resorts

WOOF for Petco

FIZZ for National Beverage Corp.

CAKE for The Cheesecake Factory

My favorite ticker symbol is UTRS, the ticker for Minerva Health, an innovative women's health company. Now that's funny.

Using Ticker Symbols

Ticker symbols are used in brokerage accounts to research a stock, get a price quote, and to trade.

While you can use a company's full name, its ticker symbol works better. For example, if you want to research American Express, type its ticker – AXP – into the search bar. The company pops up.

If you don't have the ticker symbol and type "American," all sorts of things pop up – American Eagle, American Airlines, American Century Equity Fund. You get the idea.

Though it will feel awkward at first, get in the habit of using ticker symbols.

Use Google to learn the ticker symbol for any company that interests you.

Try It!

This chapter ends with a challenge. Go to Yahoo! Finance (www.yahoo.com → Finance) and enter ticker symbols from this chapter (TAP, WOOF, CAKE). Do this before reading further.

The more you engage, the more you will learn.

Chapter 3

Why Did That Stock Price Move?

No introduction to stocks is complete without discussing their volatility. If you plan to invest in individual stocks, then prepare for a roller coaster ride. Stocks lose value quickly and recover slowly. They confound investors.

Uber reached $60 a share in 2021. One year later its stock was $20. Now it's above $50.

Meta, the parent company of Facebook and Instagram, climbed to almost $400 a share in 2021. By 2022, its stock was $90. Now it's $330.

Netflix briefly touched $700 a share in 2021 then plummeted to under $200 by April 2022. The subscription streaming service recovered in 2023 but remains well below its high.

In the past few years, many popular stocks experienced big price swings. Why is the stock market so dramatic?

Diagnosis

One could argue the stock market suffers from bipolar disorder. It is too high when it is high, and too low when it is low.

Benjamin Graham, the father of value investing, was the first to popularize this mood disorder concept. In his best-selling book, *The Intelligent Investor*, Graham created the character "Mr. Market," a fellow who periodically offers to buy your stake in a business for a price that is very pessimistic or wildly optimistic.

Mr. Market became a famous allegory.

Supply and Demand

Before we throw up our hands and pronounce the stock market mentally ill, there are some logical and objective reasons stock prices fluctuate.

Stock prices, like all prices, are impacted by supply and demand. Since supply is mostly steady, we'll start with the demand side of the equation.

No question, demand is often driven by company earnings. However, a myriad of factors like world events, inflation, insider selling, algorithmic trading, and investor sentiment can move a stock's price, especially in the short-term.

These factors fall into the following categories:

Fundamentals

Macroeconomics

Behavioral Finance

Technical Analysis

Other factors

Fundamentals

Sales, profit, debt level, and leadership are examples of fundamentals. They are the core features of a business.

Chief among these is profit, also known as earnings, or what's left after expenses have been paid. "Ultimately the earnings will decide the fate of a stock," declared Peter Lynch in his best-selling book, *One Up on Wall Street*.

Investors have been known to panic when profits decline or a decline is forecast. In November 2023, Petco lowered its earnings guidance for the year and the stock dropped 30% in a matter of hours.

Macroeconomics

Stocks exist in a macro environment that can lift or sink them.

Listen to any podcast on investing and the talk will likely cover interest rates, inflation, and employment statistics. These are a few examples of macroeconomic factors.

Macro trends matter because they impact a company's fundamentals. For example, if interest rates rise, then companies pay more to borrow money. Higher borrowing costs mean lower profits.

Especially in the short term, anything from geopolitical unrest (think war in Ukraine) to higher inflation can impact stock prices.

Buy, Sell or Hold ratings by Wall Street analysts typically incorporate both fundamental analysis and macroeconomic factors. These ratings can move a stock's price.

Behavioral Finance

People are swayed by emotions and biases. Investors buy a stock with lousy fundamentals because others are buying it (herd instinct). They fail to consider attractive investments overseas (home country bias). Many ignore bargain prices because recent market declines feel more real than prior market advances (recency bias).

While Behavioral Finance is a relatively new field in academia, the notion that people allow their emotions to impact their decisions is not new. In 1936, famous British economist John Maynard Keynes coined the term **animal spirits** to identify how emotions impact our economic choices.

More recently, meme stocks (stocks that "go viral") took the herd instinct to new heights with FOMO, the fear of missing out.

Technical Analysis

One takeaway from the best-selling book *A Random Walk Down Wall Street* is that technical analysis is controversial. Some swear by it (the technicians). Some swear at it (*Random Walk* author Burton Malkiel and others).

Technical analysis tracks the movement of a stock's price and the volume of shares traded. Technicians scrutinize price charts and look for specific patterns that suggest the future trajectory of the stock.

It's difficult in a book to convey the extent to which day traders and technicians rely on price charts. If you are interested in technical analysis, go to YouTube, and, in the search bar, enter "Basics of candlesticks" (yes, "candlesticks." They are the graphic representation of price movements on price charts). There is no shortage of "experts" who want to share these patterns with you.

Other

Not all phenomena that move a stock's price fit neatly into one of the categories above. Here are additional factors that deserve mention.

Algorithmic trading – some investment firms devise computer programs that buy and sell stocks under pre-set conditions. These fully automated investing strategies can move a stock's price if the volume is significant.

Added/Removed from an index –In September 2023, Newell Brands, the maker of Quickie mops, saw its stock price drop when it was removed from the S&P 500 Index. Conversely, private equity firm Blackstone saw its shares rise when it was added to the index. Indexes are covered later in this book.

Cyberattack – Bleach isn't boring when cybersecurity is threatened. In the Fall of 2023, stock in Clorox declined significantly when the company was hit by a cyberattack.

The dividend – Any increase or decrease in a company's dividend can move its stock price (see "Dividends" in the chapter, "Evaluating a Stock").

Insider buying/selling – Company officers must disclose to the public when they buy or sell their company's stock. Purchases are seen as a good sign and selling is seen as a negative indicator.

Short covering/Short squeeze – A complicated situation that can temporarily boost demand for an out-of-favor stock. Investors short a stock by borrowing shares, selling them, then repurchasing them when it is time to return the borrowed shares.

Shorting is risky because short sellers can lose a lot of money if share prices climb. Investors "cover" their short position by buying, which could create a spike in price. The GameStop frenzy was partly the result of short covering.

Tax loss harvesting – Stocks that are down for the year can continue to decline because investors are selling shares to capture a loss. From a tax perspective, realized losses are valuable because they can offset realized gains (see the chapter, "The Tax Consequences of Investing").

The Supply Side

While the supply side (i.e., the number of shares outstanding) is mostly steady, companies do issue new stock or take current stock out of circulation (share buybacks). Increased supply typically lowers a stock's price and decreased supply raises it.

Conclusion

The next time your favorite stock jumps or plummets, return to this chapter and try to find the cause. Or you can just think, "That's crazy." You won't be alone.

Chapter 4

Evaluating a Stock

The chapter, "What Is a Stock?" opened with this question:

Which of these two scenarios best describes you?

Scenario A: The Hoka running shoe is a hot new trend. Everyone is buying them. You buy a pair, too.

Scenario B: The Hoka running shoe is a hot new trend. Everyone is buying them. You buy shares in the company that makes Hokas.

If this passage struck you as a call to buy Deckers Brands, the maker of Hokas, or to buy the stocks behind hot trends in general, then we need to talk.

Trends can age well or poorly. Starbucks nailed the premium coffee trend. According to *The Motley Fool*, a popular investing website, an investment of $10,000 in the Starbucks IPO in 1992 was worth over $4 million by 2021.

On the flip side, Beyond Meat, the most popular company riding the plant-based meat trend, has disappointed investors. Anyone who bought Beyond Meat's stock at its high has lost over 90%.

Missed it?

One smart real estate investor observed, "You make all your money on the buy." She meant that getting a good price is the key to making money. The same is true for stocks.

Going back to those Hokas, its stock (ticker symbol: DECK) climbed from $170 in 2020 to over $600 in 2023. Anyone who noticed the Hokas trend early and acted quickly was rewarded.

Now the price is too high in terms of one critical measure: the price-to-earnings ratio (P/E ratio).

P/E ratio

Objective measurements underpin thoughtful evaluation.

Just like a scale measures weight and a ruler measures length, stock charts give you the P/E ratio to gauge whether a stock is expensive.

P/E stands for price-to-earnings. The P/E ratio compares a stock's price to its earnings-per-share (EPS). For example, if a company has a stock price of $20 and EPS of $2, then its P/E ratio is 10.

When the P/E ratio of DECK is compared to P/Es of other publicly traded footwear companies, Deckers Brands falls somewhere between fairly valued to over-valued.

Company:	Ticker:	P/E ratio:
Deckers Brands	DECK	30
Crocs	CROX	10
Sketchers	SKX	17
Nike	NKE	35

This is no knock on Hokas. The DECK P/E is reasonable compared to many hot stocks like Nvidia (P/E 60) and Tesla (P/E 77).

There's something about the lure of innovation that makes investors lose their heads.

Just don't lose yours.

As Peter Lynch advises in his best-selling book, *One Up on Wall Street*, "If you remember nothing else about P/E ratios, remember to avoid stocks with excessively high ones."

Fun with Financial Statements

Imagine you are on a blind date with an exceedingly attractive person who is a good talker. You are having a terrific time.

What if, before you got too hooked, you could access this person's college transcript, work history, credit score, medical records, the works. Wouldn't it be helpful to get past external good looks to what's underneath?

Well, when you flirt with the idea of buying a stock, you can.

Public companies are required by law to regularly disclose information like sales, earnings, debt level, and business risk factors. These disclosures are included in the 10-Qs (quarterly reports) and 10-K (Annual Report) which are filed with the Securities and Exchange Commission (SEC), the government agency in charge of protecting investors. Copies of these reports are typically found on a company's website in the Investor Relations section.

Among these disclosures are three financial statements:

The Income Statement

The Balance Sheet

The Statement of Cash Flows

If you are serious about investing in individual stocks, then you must learn to read these statements. Numerous YouTube videos are available to help you get started. Select one of these statements and enter it in the YouTube search bar (e.g., enter "the balance sheet").

Shortcuts

While diligent investors review financial statements, you can use shortcuts.

Many public libraries subscribe to services like Value Line that independently analyze and rate stocks. Check out the free resources at your library.

Similarly, as you will see in the section of this book that covers bonds, there are bond ratings agencies that perform lengthy due diligence to evaluate public companies. You can use bond ratings in place of your own homework (see the chapter, "Evaluating a Bond"). This shortcut only works if the company issues bonds.

Dividends

Recall from the chapter, "The Language of Investing," that professional money managers segment the universe of investable stocks into either "growth" or "value." While Wall Street favors growth, those in the value camp have an entirely different mindset for what makes a good stock.

Value investors love established companies that reward investors with dividends. Dividends are periodic cash payments issued to stockholders. Here are some examples:

Company	Dividend
IBM	$1.66 per share, quarterly
Pfizer	$0.41 per share, quarterly
Ford	$0.15 per share, quarterly

For some, dividend income is the secret sauce of stock returns. As legendary investor John Bogle noted in his book, *Enough*, dividends accounted for almost half of all stock investment gains from 1900 to 2007.

Depending on the price of a share of stock, dividends can match the yield of a bank certificate of deposit (CD) with the upside potential of the stock price increasing.

In general, value investors love dividends, low P/Es, and solid bond ratings.

Second-level Thinking

Acclaimed investor Howard Marks has made billions in profits for his clients. In his book, *The Most Important Thing*, Marks urges investors to adopt "second-level thinking." Here's an excerpt from his book:

First-level thinking says, "It's a good company; let's buy the stock." Second-level thinking says, "It's a good company, but everyone thinks it's a great company, and it's not. The stock is overrated and overpriced; let's sell."

In the final analysis, picking a stock goes beyond the fundamentals. You must have an edge over other investors. After all, there's someone on the other side of every stock trade who is making the opposite move. Are you sure you are smarter?

We'll discuss this question further in the chapters on strategy.

Chapter 5

What Is a Bond?

Bonds had a dismal year in 2022. If you heard about the carnage, then you may wonder why bonds are worth your time.

Investors have a bad habit of avoiding investments that decline and chasing ones that soar. This is the opposite of the maxim, "Buy low and sell high."

Now is the perfect time to learn about bonds. The high-quality ones offer a solid return with low risk.

What is a bond?

Corporations, governments, school districts, and other entities issue bonds when they want to borrow money. Think of a bond as a large loan with very specific details like its interest rate (called the coupon rate) and the date the loan will be repaid (the maturity date).

Just to confuse you, bonds are not always called bonds. Loans to the U.S. government for one year or less are called "bills." Loans to the government for two to ten years are called "notes," a term also used by corporations.

As a group, bills, notes, and bonds are also called debt instruments, debt securities or fixed-income securities.

The best way to learn about these securities is to compare them. Below are several real, actively traded bonds whose differences highlight key considerations when buying debt securities.

Issuer (Borrower): Apple

Bond amount: $750,000,000

Coupon rate: 1.8%

Current yield: 1.9%

Maturity Date: 9/11/24

CUSIP: 037833DM9

Issuer (Borrower): Starbucks

Bond amount: $500,000,000

Coupon rate: 4.8%

Current Yield: 5.1%

Maturity Date: 2/15/33

CUSIP: 855244BF5

Issuer (Borrower): Ford Motor Company

Bond amount: $501,918,000

Coupon rate: 8.9%

Current Yield: 7.9%

Maturity Date: 1/15/32

CUSIP: 345370BV1

Issuer (Borrower): United States of America

Bond amount: $48,000,137,800

Coupon rate: 5.0%

Current yield: 4.7%

Maturity Date: 9/30/2025

CUSIP: 91282CJB8

Issuer (Borrower): State of Tennessee General Obligation Bonds

Bond amount: $10,775,000

Coupon rate: 5%

Current Yield: 2.8%

Maturity Date: 11/01/2029

CUSIP: 880541D20

Issuer (Borrower): Cabot Arkansas School District

Bond amount: $485,000

Coupon rate: 2.0%

Current Yield: 4.7%

Maturity Date: 2/01/2026

CUSIP: 127037UM9

As you can see, bonds are **enormous loans**. They are brought to market by underwriters (typically investment banks like Goldman Sachs or J.P Morgan) that parcel out the bond to broker-dealers and/or to institutional investors like pension funds, insurance companies, endowments, and banks. Note: The process for U.S. government bonds is different. The federal government holds auctions where multiple underwriters participate.

While many bonds never get apportioned small enough for the average investor (some bonds only sell in increments of $25,000 or more), there are high-quality bonds that you can buy in increments of $1,000.

It's the $1,000 bond that should intrigue you. They are easily purchased through online brokers, pay higher interest rates than bank CDs, and many are low-risk or risk-free.

Make sure you understand terms like coupon rate and maturity date listed below. These terms are used in the next two chapters.

Issuer (Borrower)

As you can see, bonds are issued by a wide variety of entities from corporations to governments to school districts. In fact, **the bond market is larger than the stock market.**

Bond Amount

The entire amount borrowed. Underwriters sell portions of this amount to broker-dealers and/or to institutional investors like pension funds, insurance companies, endowments, and banks.

Coupon Rate

The coupon rate is the interest rate the borrower pays on the bond. The coupon is paid at consistent intervals (most often semiannually) over the life of the bond.

Current Yield

When a bond is issued, its current yield equals its coupon rate. In the secondary market (the market where bonds trade after they have been distributed by underwriters), the price of a bond fluctuates. Price fluctuations cause the current yield to deviate from the coupon rate.

Maturity Date

The maturity date is the date the borrowed amount is paid back in full.

CUSIPs and ISINs

Bonds have unique ID numbers to prevent confusion. The CUSIP (Committee on Uniform Securities Identification Procedures) number identifies bonds registered in the U.S. and Canada.

ISIN stands for International Securities Identification Number which – you guessed it! – identifies bonds issued outside the U.S. and Canada. For example, the Republic of Ireland issued a bond for $8 billion Euros. The ISIN for the bond is IE00B6X95T99.

Sign Me Up!

Among the bonds listed above, Ford's bond offers the highest current yield at 7.9%. If you noticed that and thought, "No brainer, buy that one," think again.

The idea that bonds are safe is a persistent myth. Only some bonds are safe. Others are very risky.

The next two chapters discuss the price volatility of bonds and how to pick the best ones based on your risk tolerance.

Chapter 6

Bond Prices

In his book, *Bonds: An Introduction to Core Concepts,* Mark Mobius had this to say about their popularity: "One reason is that, unlike stocks, they allow investors to sleep at night because there are no stomach-churning, roller coaster rides in prices to worry about."

If you noted the steep losses in bonds last year, then this assertion seems false. However, you and Mark Mobius are both right.

High-quality bonds purchased at or near their issuance date and held to maturity are sleepy safe. They only cause trouble if an investor wants to sell the bond. Take Apple's bond, for example.

Issuer (Borrower): Apple

Bond amount: $750,000,000

Coupon rate: 1.8%

Current yield: 1.9%

Yield to maturity: 5%

Maturity Date: 9/11/24

CUSIP: 037833DM9

Apple issued this bond on September 4, 2019. The company borrowed money at a very low rate of interest for two reasons: prevailing interest rates were low at that time, and Apple is considered one of the most creditworthy companies in the U.S.

Today, the coupon on this bond is not competitive (to say the least). The yield on a U.S. Treasury bill that matures in one year is 5%. Because Treasuries are backed by the full faith and credit of the U.S. government, their yields are considered the **risk-free rate.**

If the holder of an Apple bond wants to sell, who will buy the bond when Treasuries yielding 5% are risk-free, plentiful, and easily purchased?

Discount Bonds

To sell the Apple bond prior to its maturity date, the holder must accept a lower price than what she paid at issuance. The lower price **creates a yield** that is competitive with market conditions.

For example, if she has $1,000 worth of the Apple bond, she can create a 5% yield by selling the bond for $970.

Do not tune out because of math! Stay with me to grasp the logic.

On September 11, 2024, the Apple bond matures. Whoever holds the bond on that date receives the original principal amount – not what they paid – for the bond.

In this case, the bondholder who paid $970 will get $1,000. The extra $30, added to the 1.8% coupon payments, brings the yield to maturity of the bond to 5%. The bond is now competitive with U.S. Treasuries.

Bonds that sell for less than their issue price are discount bonds. Bonds that sell for more than their issue price are premium bonds.

Premium Bonds

In the example above, the bond price was lowered to make the bond yield higher. Bond prices also increase, which makes the yield lower.

Clearly, lower yields are not something bondholders want; they are at the mercy of market conditions. Take the Ford bond, for example.

Issuer (Borrower): Ford Motor Company

Bond amount: $501,918,000

Coupon rate: 8.9%

Current Yield: 7.9%

Maturity Date: 1/15/32

CUSIP: 345370BV1

The Ford bond was issued on June 4, 1998, with a coupon rate of 8.9% and a maturity date more than 30 years in the future.

Ford is still paying 8.9% (remember, the coupon rate never changes). This means Ford pays $89 per year for every $1,000 it borrowed.

The current yield on the Ford bond is 7.9% which means the current price of the bond must be higher than the original price.

Again, don't zone out due to math.

Bond buyers today pay $1,120 for $1,000 worth of the original Ford bond. $89 (the annual coupon payment) is 7.9% of $1,120.

Ford is a premium bond because its current price is higher than its original price.

Bondholder Blues

CNBC, the cable channel devoted to investing, ran this headline on its website: "2022 was the worst-ever year for U.S. bonds." The headline sounds so dire you might think everyone owns the Apple bond with a measly 1.8% coupon.

The truth is no one loses money unless they sell. This is a key point, especially if your mother or grandmother owns bonds that mature decades into the future.

On paper, bonds with distant maturities got pummeled in 2022 because prevailing interest rates rose to levels not seen in years. But no one can predict the future. As of this writing, interest rates have already reversed and headed lower.

Rule #1

If you take away nothing else from this chapter, remember this: interest rates and bond prices have an inverse relationship.

When interest rates rise, bond prices fall. When interest rates fall, bond prices rise.

Chapter 7

Evaluating a Bond

Considering the impact of interest rates on bond prices, you might guess that predicting the direction of interest rates is the first step in evaluating a bond.

Don't bother, says longtime money manager John Spooner. In his book, *No One Ever Told Us That*, Spooner says people waste an inordinate amount of time on interest rate forecasts. No one knows the direction of interest rates.

Focus on what you can control.

Buying a bond makes you a lender. Smart lenders only give money to creditworthy borrowers.

How can you make sure a bond issuer is creditworthy? Just like you, bonds have a credit score. In the bond world, this score is called a rating, and it's a letter grade rather than a number.

Bond Ratings

Moody's, S&P Global, and Fitch are the most well-known bond rating agencies. They conduct thorough reviews of bond issuers.

Here are their ratings for the companies from the first bond chapter:

Bond	Moody's	S&P Global	Fitch
Apple	Aaa	AA+	N/A
Starbucks	Baa1	BBB+	BBB
Ford	Ba1	BBB-	BBB-

Source: Fidelity Brokerage. Fitch website.

Bs are fine on a report card, but they are not good for bonds. According to bond expert Mark Mobius, Moody's Ba1 rating – the rating on the Ford bond – is *ten notches* below its top rating (best to worst is Aaa, Aa1, Aa2, Aa3, A1, A2, A3, Baa1, Baa2, Baa3, Ba1 and down).

Even worse, Ba1 is considered below investment grade. In other words, a junk bond. Ford is considered split rated since it has one rating at investment grade and one below.

High yield

Bonds with lower credit quality typically offer higher coupon rates. Some people jump at the chance of higher yields and ignore the risk that the bond issuer will fail to pay interest or return principal at the bond's maturity (a.k.a. default).

Low yield

High-yield (junk) bonds may be risky, but low-yield bonds just seem dumb. Why would anyone settle for a low yield if he can buy a high-quality bond with a higher one?

Some bonds are exempt from federal and state income taxes. For investors in high tax brackets (think Taylor Swift and Travis Kelce), bonds with **favorable tax treatment** are a better deal than taxable bonds with higher yields. These bonds are municipal bonds or "muni" bonds.

Most people don't need bonds with special tax treatment but, if you took mom's advice and majored in STEM or headed to Wall Street, then you may land in a tax bracket that makes them worthwhile.

Baby steps

OK. You don't have a brokerage account or much money or time to investigate bond ratings. But you want to get started. Check out I Bonds at treasurydirect.gov (that's the letter "I." Government savings bonds start with letters).

You can purchase I Bonds for as little as $25.

I Bonds currently yield 5.27%, the interest grows tax free, and you pay no state or local tax when you cash in the bond. If you use the accrued interest for education purposes, you pay no tax at all (unless you have a relatively high income).

Solid yield, no risk, maybe no taxes. Told you reading this book would be fun.

Chapter 8

Mutual Funds

For most investors, all you need are mutual funds.

-Rob Berger, *Forbes* Contributor

Mutual funds pool money from a group of investors to buy a variety of securities. They are the investment of choice in employer-sponsored retirement plans.

Mutual funds can be laser-focused like the Hennessy Gas Utility Fund, which only invests in natural gas companies, or broadly focused like the Vanguard Total Bond Market Index Fund, that provides wide exposure to U.S. investment-grade bonds. They can include only stocks or bonds or mix them together.

Mutual Funds have the odd distinction of being both ubiquitous and endangered. They dominate 401(k) investment options, and your grandmother's portfolio, but they are declining in popularity.

Without a brief history lesson, this decline is hard to explain. Back in the day, investors had to purchase stocks in "round lots" of 100 shares and commissions on trades were 8% (yes! 8%).

Today, through *fractional* shares (literally a fraction of one share of stock) and zero commission trades, anyone can create their own mutual fund instantly for less than $1,000.

Mutual funds seem as necessary as a coal stove when you own a microwave.

Still, cold pizza never tastes quite right warmed in a microwave, and mutual funds have one enduring advantage: you can't sell them during the trading day. If one key to investing success is to stay the course, then it's a good thing that several steps are needed to sell a mutual fund.

Here's how to find information on mutual funds in your employer-sponsored plan or ones that otherwise interest you.

Ticker Symbol

Ticker Symbols for mutual funds are always five letters. For example:

Mutual Fund	Ticker
Hennessy Gas Utility Fund	GASFX
Vanguard Total Bond Market Index Fund	VBTLX
Fidelity Mid Cap Value Fund	FSMVX

There are thousands of funds with similar names. It's essential to use ticker symbols to investigate the mutual funds offered in your 401(k) plan or to review ones that interest you.

Index Funds

Index is another one of those financial words you can't infer from its everyday meaning. When you see the word "index" in a fund, think "group" or "sub-group" and then think "average."

For example, fund managers that target mid-cap companies can either actively research them and select the best ones, or they can buy all mid-cap companies and accept the average result of how they perform.

If aiming for average sounds boring and lazy, you'd be shocked to learn that experts favor this approach. This is the "active versus passive" debate, a.k.a. the "you can't beat the market" assertion.

In any case, when you see the word "index" in a fund name, it means the entire group or sub-group is represented, no cherry-picking.

Target-date funds

Over the years, investors are supposed to lower their investment risk by reducing stocks and adding high-quality bonds. The logic is that an older investor cannot weather a dramatic stock market decline too close to retirement.

Target-date funds are the set-it-and-forget-it strategy on steroids. They manage the multi-decade risk-reduction process for you.

But are they worth the extra cost? Doesn't seem too difficult to sell some S&P 500 Index Fund and buy the Total Bond Market every three years.

Fees

There's a reason "fees" is a four-letter word. It is the worst kind of pest: Hard to find and resistant to eradication. Look for fees under "expense ratio" in fund information.

Unsuspecting investors get gouged by fees they could easily avoid. It's as if they don't understand that a 1% fee on an investment that earns 5% is *20% of the entire gain*.

Vanguard, the asset manager famous for low fees, usually has a fund identical to whichever fund wants to charge you too much. Shop wisely.

<u>Try It!</u>

Here's another challenge. Go to Google and enter ticker symbols from this chapter (GASFX, VBTLX, FSMVX). Do this before reading further.

Your search should lead to links to key fund disclosures (top holdings, fees, performance), and to Morningstar reviews. Morningstar offers valuable independent analysis of funds.

Chapter 9

Exchange-Traded Funds

Many of the newest ETFs are bad investments, pure and simple. They were introduced to take advantage of the popularity of ETFs. They are overly expensive, and they represent foolish indexes (extremely small segments of the market, or indexes constructed using highly questionable methodologies).

-Russell Wild, *ETFs for Dummies*

Many financial professionals will tell you that exchange-traded funds (ETFs) are basically mutual funds that trade during the day. Not exactly. A mutual fund owns the securities in its fund.

An ETF has a claim on a basket of securities sort of like you have a claim on your coat when the coat check lady gives you a ticket.

Paranoid people pause on this point. Just thought you should know.

Having said this, ETFs caught on for good reasons. Eric Balchunas, the senior ETF analyst at Bloomberg, compared mutual funds and ETFs and concluded, "You sort of see the ETF as taking a few evolutionary steps forward." They provide greater tax efficiency and trade during the day.

It's fair to say ETFs are a popular trend, and, like any popular trend, you get low-quality knockoffs. Unscrupulous financial folks create ETFs with catchy ticker symbols and compelling themes like saving the planet. These ETFs come with hefty hidden fees and questionable portfolio management (they also come with legal teams that can squash authors which is why no specific examples are given).

Slick marketers are not the only problem with ETFs. Liquidity is a serious issue.

Liquidity is a measure of how easily an asset can be bought or sold. Your parents' house might be worth a bundle, but it is an illiquid asset. It takes months to sell a house. Meanwhile, the stock of most publicly traded companies is highly liquid.

Bonds range from highly liquid to illiquid, but all bond ETFs act like liquidity isn't an issue.

Beware of bond ETFs if investors sour on bonds all at once. The price of your bond ETF could nosedive.

The conservative approach is to only buy ETFs that track highly liquid markets like mid to large-cap stocks. And you always check for hidden fees now, right?

Chapter 10

Cryptocurrency

It's January 19, 2023, and Jim Cramer is furious. "If you are a believer in crypto, this is your chance to become a non-believer," he declares on his TV show, *Mad Money*. "It's a travesty of a mockery of a sham, and it's manipulated, and I've had it, and I want you out."

Did we mention cryptocurrencies are controversial?

In 2017, Bitcoin, the world's most popular cryptocurrency, became a sensation by rising over 2,000% in less than a year. Then Bitcoin's price dropped abruptly. By November 2018, Bitcoin was down 80% from its high.

This dramatic boom-and-bust cycle was repeated. At the time

of Cramer's rant, Bitcoin had fallen 77% from a high of 68,789 in November 2021 to a low of 15,599 in 2022.

Many financial experts are so exasperated by the wild price swings of Bitcoin and its ilk that they recommend you avoid crypto entirely.

Not so fast. Cryptocurrencies remain intriguing because of the unique problems they aim to solve.

Innovation

Before Bitcoin, savvy tech experts bemoaned the limits of fiat currency. Government-controlled money isn't suited to the digital world, they said. Visionaries longed for a currency that was decentralized, digital, borderless, anonymous, and peer-to-peer.

Bitcoin addressed these needs with nerdy elegance. Satoshi Nakamoto's white paper (Satoshi Nakamoto is presumed to be a pseudonym) caused a sensation.

Bitcoin is not a scam; it's an innovation, and many of today's most popular cryptocurrencies are attempts to improve on Bitcoin. For example, Solana (SOL) skyrocketed in 2023 because it is "much faster and cheaper to run transactions on than Bitcoin...," according to Bloomberg Markets editor Michael Regan.

Having said this, Bitcoin and up-and-coming cryptos are beyond the scope of this book.

Speculation

Cryptocurrencies are not covered in any depth in this book because they are not "investments." As Benjamin Graham noted in *The Intelligent Investor*, "An investment operation is one which, upon thorough analysis, promises safety of principal and an adequate return. Operations not meeting these requirements are speculative."

Some cryptocurrencies deserve your respect, and they might deserve a place in your portfolio.

Time will tell.

Chapter 11

How to Buy Investments

There are reasons you don't buy groceries at a convenience store: The selection is poor, and the prices are too high. The same could be said for investments. The familiar spot on the corner is not the right place to buy them. Consider this true story.

Forget the Bank

Brian (not his real name) decided it was time to get serious about investing. He made an appointment with his local bank. He assumed the bank was the right place to start.

The bank representative suggested a mutual fund that tracked an unusual sector of the stock market and charged a hefty fee of 5% (called a "load," this term basically means sales commission).

Luckily Brian was skeptical and held on to his money.

Brokers

If you want a wide selection of investments at low cost, then shop at a DISCOUNT broker.

Brokerage firms act as the intermediaries between buyers and sellers of securities. Discount Brokers have a low-cost, self-serve model whereas full-service brokers charge you for investment advice.

If you have a valid social security number and a bank account, an account at a brokerage is easy to open, and you can do it online.

Keep thinking groceries

Remember those unscrupulous marketers from the ETF section? Well, their cousins all started financial apps that lure you with game-like features or gimmicks like a free share of stock.

Ignore them! You want the equivalent of Costco or Safeway or Hannaford: big, well-established discount brokers that come highly recommended by friends and co-workers.

Or take Emma's advice. Emma Goodness, a junior at Tulane University, researched online brokers for her summer internship. She found that Fidelity, Schwab, and E-trade are the best ones for young adults who are just getting started.

Is your money safe?

Bernie Madoff. Silicon Valley Bank. Sam Bankman Fried. There is no shortage of headlines to make us wonder if our money is safe.

Good news! Several agencies protect your money.

The Federal Deposit Insurance Corporation (FDIC) was established by Congress to maintain stability and public confidence in the nation's financial system. FDIC covers your bank account.

The Securities and Exchange Commission (SEC) has broad authority to protect investors and to maintain fair, orderly, and efficient markets.

The Securities Investor Protection Corporation (SIPC) protects investors from certain types of losses (think broker goes bankrupt or steals your money).

Though SIPC protection covers "only" $500,000 (with a cap of $250,000 on cash) folks burned by Bernie Madoff received substantially more than that. The SIPC website reports that "Any customer with a net asset value of up to approximately $1.705 million was made whole."

While the SIPC has your back if your broker goes bankrupt, FINRA polices brokers behaving badly. For example, FINRA (the Financial Industry Regulatory Authority) stepped in when a broker made 700 trades in the account of a 77-year-old blind widow.

You can also vet brokers online using FINRA's BrokerCheck or call the BrokerCheck help line at (800) 289-9999

Now will you sleep better at night?

Chapter 12

The Tax Consequences of Investing

Imagine you buy 50 shares of Peloton stock. Over the next several months, the shares decline. You are discouraged and decide to sell. Two weeks later the high-tech fitness company reports good news, and the stock starts to climb. Now you have FOMO. You repurchase the stock.

Congratulations! You just ran afoul of the "Wash-sale Rule."

The wash-sale rule prohibits selling an investment for a loss and replacing it with the same or "substantially identical" investment **30 days before or after the sale.**

If you trigger a wash sale, you will not be allowed to deduct your investment losses. Normally, your losses can be used to offset investment gains elsewhere.

As you can see, tax ignorance is costly. On the flip side, it also robs you of valuable benefits. Most people have no idea they can avoid paying tax on I Bond interest if they use it to pay for qualified education expenses. They would choose the I Bond over other investments if they understood the obscure tax rule.

This chapter aims to both caution and alert you. In the tax world, mundane actions can lead to costly consequences, and tax cluelessness can cause you to miss opportunities.

Disclaimer

This chapter is for educational and informational purposes only. It is not intended to provide financial, legal, tax or investment advice.

Before you buy or sell any investment, you are urged to consult a tax professional who is aware of your unique situation.

Prerequisite: Taxes 101

To grasp the tax consequences of investing, you must understand that ours is a progressive tax system (the higher your taxable income the greater *percentage* you pay in tax). If you are fuzzy on this topic, then email: questions@moneyinyourtwenties.com to request a FREE copy of "Taxes 101."

Gains are taxed!

The long arm of the tax man comes as a shock to many young adults. They know they owe taxes on income from work, but they are surprised when they owe taxes on bank account interest, their side hustle, and winning bets on DraftKings.

Ditto investment income. Unless your money is in a tax shelter, taxes are owed on interest and dividend income and on "capital gains" (the difference in the amount you paid for a security and the amount you received when you sold it, assuming you sold for a gain).

No, Low or High Tax

In numerous scenarios, two considerations determine whether you owe no tax, low tax, or high tax:

Where your money is held

Whether ordinary income or capital gains rates apply

Where your money is held

As a society, we value education and saving for the future. Our tax laws reflect these values. Investors can defer and/or eliminate taxes with legal tax shelters like the 401(k), IRA, and 529 Plan.

The 401(k) is named after the subsection of the U.S. Tax Code that created it. 401(k)s allow workers to defer taxes on a portion of their pay and allow investments to grow tax free.

403(b) plans are the same as 401(k) plans except they are offered to government employees and workers at non-profit organizations.

Roth 401(k)s are funded with after-tax dollars. With a Roth, you skip the immediate tax break offered through a regular 401(k). However, you **pay no tax** when you finally access the money after age 59 ½.

IRAs are Individual Retirement Accounts. A regular IRA has the same tax advantages as a 401(k) and a Roth IRA has the same tax advantages as a Roth 401(k).

529 plans (state-sponsored college savings plans) allow contributions to grow tax-free and gains are not taxed if used for qualified education expenses.

Ordinary Income or Capital Gains Rates

Ordinary income rates (those tax brackets in our progressive system you are supposed to already understand) start small – 10% and 12% – and then jump up to 22% depending on your income. Worst-case scenario is 37%, the top bracket.

Capital gains rates start at 0%. Most gains are taxed at 15%. The upper limit is 20%.

Clearly capital gains rates are preferable, and it is your job to learn the rules that push you out of the good camp and into the costly one. For example, if you realize a "short-term" gain on an investment (meaning you owned the investment for one year or less), ordinary income rates apply. If you hold the investment longer, then capital gains rates apply.

The Internal Revenue Service (IRS) creates publications that list current tax rules. You can download the one on investment income – Publication 550 – at IRS.gov.

Publication 550 is 75 pages of tiny font and tedious reading. Your friend the tycoon (37% tax bracket) is so freaked out by ordinary income rates that she gave up on Pub. 550 and hired a tax pro. Here's how you can, too.

Hiring a tax professional

Any reputable tax preparer will have a Preparer Tax Identification Number (PTIN). This number is required by the Internal Revenue Service (IRS). Do not hire anyone who lacks this basic credential.

Avoid tax preparers who claim they can get you a large refund. Do not use tax preparers who base their fee on the size of the refund.

As your tax situation gets more complicated, you will want someone who can represent you before the IRS. Ask co-workers, friends, and family if they know a reputable Enrolled Agent. They are less expensive than tax attorneys and can speak to the IRS on your behalf.

Certified Public Accountants can also represent you before the IRS. They are typically more expensive than Enrolled Agents.

Chapter 13

Strategy, Part I

Investing is all about taking steps today
to take care of yourself in the future;
it's really the greatest act of self-care you can practice.

– Tiffany Aliche, *Get Good with Money*

Is financial success as simple as skipping Starbucks? David Bach drew flack for making this claim in his book, *The Latte Factor*. In protest, financial industry critic Helaine Olen titled a chapter of her book "The Latte is a Lie." Another writer titled her book, *Eat the Avocado Toast,* boldly claiming that frugality is the wrong approach to succeed with money.

Though controversial, Bach has a valid and timeless message: small changes can create remarkable results.

Don't worry, you don't have to give up Starbucks. "The latte factor is a metaphor," explains Henry, a fictional character in Bach's book. "It could be anything you spend extra money on that you could happily do without. Cigarettes. A candy bar. Fancy cocktails. Anything."

James Clear, the author of the best-selling book *Atomic Habits*, agrees that small changes are important because they "compound into remarkable results."

Use any savings calculator on the internet – Bankrate.com has a good one – and you see the power of compounding. In 20 years, **saving only $100 a month at 8% interest becomes $57,366.00.** Financial professionals like to call this, "the miracle of compound interest."

However, compounding is no miracle when the only thing compounding is the interest on your debt. That's why you need small changes and *a smart strategy.*

Many young adults today must weigh the benefits of saving and investing against the goal of paying off student loans. If you have credit card debt, eliminating it is a more urgent matter than anything else.

While no rules are etched in stone and each person's situation is unique (that's the "personal" in "personal finance"), the remainder of this chapter could help you to prioritize your money moves.

Recommended sequence of money moves

1. Contribute to 401(k) *if employer offers a match*

2. Pay off credit card debt

3. Contribute to a 401(k), Roth 401(k) or Roth IRA

4. Build an emergency fund

5. Invest in yourself (networking, training, dressing for success)

6. Pay down debt

7. Insurance check-up

8. Regular savings

Contribute to 401(k) *if employer offers a match*

The chapter, "The Tax Consequences of Investing" explains the benefits of a 401(k). Contribute to get the match. There's nothing better than free money.

Pay off credit card debt

If your employer does not match your 401(k) contributions, then paying off credit cards is your #1 priority. Borrowing money at a rate of 18 - 25% is ludicrous.

Contribute to 401(k), Roth 401(k) or Roth IRA

Once you have eliminated credit card debt, start contributing to your 401(k), Roth 401(k) or Roth IRA.

Build an emergency fund

An emergency fund allows you to manage mishaps without incurring credit card debt. The amount you should save depends on how easily you can replace your income if you lose your job.

Invest in yourself (networking, training, dressing for success)

If you can **increase your income** through networking, training, or dressing for success, then it's time to invest in you. Would taking that pro to lunch get you a higher paying job? Could a public speaking class get you a promotion? Does your wardrobe reflect your real worth? Very often you are your best investment.

Pay down loans

Look at the interest rate you are charged on loans (car, student, or personal) and pay down the loan with the highest rate first. Alternatively, you can try the "snowball method."

Debt-busting guru Dave Ramsey swears by the snowball method where you ignore interest rates and pay off your smallest loan first. He argues that eliminating a loan will motivate you to pay down loans faster.

Insurance check-up

If you don't have health insurance, then drop everything, and get it. One minor health setback can devastate your finances. If you have health coverage, then renters insurance is worth a look. It's cheap, easy to buy, and protects you against theft, fire, and bad luck like a pipe bursting in the apartment above yours.

Regular savings

If you decided to live with mom and dad after college and have no student loans, then you are ready to save inside and outside a retirement account.

The next chapter discusses how to invest your savings.

Chapter 14

Strategy, Part II

Think back to high school. Who were the best athletes in your class? Now ask yourself what would happen if you tried to compete against them.

You would lose.

Remember this when you open a brokerage account. Buying a hot stock or cryptocurrency is the same as yelling, "Race you to the other side of the pool!" to an All-American swimmer.

Short-term investing is dominated by experienced day- and swing-traders who will gladly take your money. They are on the other side of hype-fueled trades.

This is not to say you should fear investing. Below is your practical guide to selecting investments **for the long-term.**

The active versus passive debate

It's time for another history lesson.

Fifty years ago, John Bogle, the father of index funds, started a revolution. He boldly rescued investors from exorbitant fees and other bad practices like "churn" (unnecessary trading in a portfolio) that harmed investors with costly tax consequences.

Index funds (see definition in the chapter on Mutual Funds) brought transparency and low cost to investing. They have boomed in popularity, and Bogle became a hero (This is not hyperbole. Bogle has a huge fan club, the Bogleheads, that produces an excellent podcast and holds an annual conference!).

But things have gone too far. Many experts advise investors to only use index funds, claiming that selecting individual securities on their merits (i.e., what active fund managers do) doesn't work.

Now there is a vocal debate among financial professionals about active versus passive money management. The active camp defends the careful selection of securities while the passive folks say you can't beat the market, just buy everything in the group or subgroup.

This book would double in size if all the pros and cons of active versus passive investing were explored. Suffice it to say that low-cost, actively managed funds have their place, as does individual stock-picking.

And index funds have flaws. America's favorite investment – the S&P 500 Index Fund – has a problem because it is usually cap-weighted. Investors buy the S&P 500 thinking they are getting a wide variety of America's top companies, but cap-weighted S&P funds favor mega-caps. As of this writing, 28% of the Vanguard S&P 500 Index Fund is only seven stocks: Apple, Microsoft, Amazon, Nvidia, Alphabet, Meta, and Berkshire Hathaway.

Benchmarks

As a smart person, you can look beyond index funds to select low-cost, actively managed funds. If you buy these funds inside a 401(k) or IRA, you have no tax consequences regardless of the fund team's trading.

Having said this, how will you know if index funds were the better choice? There are many ways to go wrong in investing. What will be your compass?

Benchmarks provide an objective measure of the market and its sub-groups.

Did you dabble in small-cap stocks? Compare your results to the Russell 2000, the small-cap U.S. stock market index.

Did you buy your first bond fund? *The Wall Street Journal* publishes a long list of bond benchmarks to guide you whether you bought a corporate or high-yield or municipal bond fund.

Behavioral Finance

Though Morgan Housel is the most popular personal finance writer of our time, he will never recommend a stock or tell you which credit card has the most rewards. Instead, Housel writes about human behavior.

"Financial success is not a hard science," says Housel in his bestseller, *The Psychology of Money.* "It's a soft skill, where how you behave is more important than what you know."

Fair point, though both knowledge and self-mastery are important.

Fingers crossed this book has helped you with both.

Epilogue

Congratulations! Now you have a solid start on your investing journey.

While you deserve a rest from all this reading, there's one more thing to mention to keep your journey safe: stranger danger.

Many people who give financial advice are "wounded healers." They completely messed up their finances and want to guide you based on nothing more than their relatable story. Run from these people.

Another group to avoid are influencers who had a few good stock picks and now want to teach you investing though they have no background in finance.

Luckily there is no shortage of excellent podcasters and writers out there. These are the folks to ask when you need directions.

The entire *Planet Money* team rocks. Start with their 2021 **Summer School** episodes. Number 5 (Bubbles, Bikes, and Biases) is pure gold.

Life Kit: Money, hosted by Chris Arnold, has a fantastic episode with David Swensen, the legendary manager of the Yale Endowment. The date is 8/21/20.

Felix Salmon at *Slate Money* has an exceptional grasp of all things financial. He's also energetic and witty. Listen and learn.

Optimal Finance Daily curates and reads the best blogs from the financial community. Start with episode #1901, Financial Locker Room Talk, by John at *ESI Money*. It teaches that anyone can call himself a "financial advisor."

If you want to get geeky, then try the September 27, 2021 episode of Chris Nelson's podcast, *The Bond Investment Mentor*. Skip the first 11 minutes, then learn all about bond yields. Brilliant.

Switching to books, Peter Lynch's *One Up on Wall Street* is my favorite, and you can't go wrong with any of these writers: Jean Chatzky, Morgan Housel, Beth Kobliner, Michelle Singletary, and Liz Weston.

If you are drowning in debt, then Dave Ramsey's book, *The Total Money Makeover*, is the next book you should read.

Well, that's a wrap. Farewell for now, dear reader. Safe travels!

Notes

Introduction

The opening paragraph describes a real brochure circulated by a top 401(k) provider. It mislabeled a junk bond fund as "conservative."

The 2023 National Report Card on States Efforts to Improve Financial Literacy in High Schools is a reputable and lengthy study by Champlain College that exposes the uneven distribution of financial literacy education in America.

Coleridge, *The Rime of the Ancient Mariner,* 1834

Podcaster quote from *The Investing for Beginners* podcast, Episode 306 ("The Bond Market Demystified"), 9/18/23. Quote is at 22:40.

Chapter 1: The Language of Investing

How to Speak Money by John Lanchester c) 2014

Market caps from Yahoo! Finance, 11/28/23

ETSY revenue from ETSY 2022 Annual Report

Rivlin quote from *Becoming a Venture Capitalist* by Gary Rivlin c) 2019, p. 6

Chapter 2: What Is a Stock?

Details on start-up financing by venture capital firms comes from *Becoming a Venture Capitalist* by Gary Rivlin c) 2019 and the 2023 Midas list by *Forbes*.

Pour Your Heart Into It by Howard Schultz c) 1999

That Will Never Work by Marc Randolph c) 2019

Instacart IPO as reported by Bloomberg Daybreak podcast on 9/19/23

Chapter 3: Why Did That Stock Price Move?

Stock prices/swings from Yahoo! Finance charts

Wikipedia used for Benjamin Graham/Mr. Market

One Up on Wall Street, Peter Lynch quote comes from pp. 163-4

Macro section drawn from astute comments by Barry Ritholtz on his *Masters in Business* podcast. His "macro-tourist" observation is hilarious

"People are swayed by emotions and biases" drawn from 6/13/15 *Masters in Business* podcast with Richard Thaler

John Maynard Keynes term "animal spirits" from Investopedia.com

Technical Analysis explanation from *A Random Walk Down Wall Street* by Burton Malkiel

Jon McAuliffe, co-founder of the Voleon Group, on the 9/8/23 episode of the podcast *Masters in Business*, explained that algorithmic trading can trigger price movement.

Yahoo! Finance reported Blackstone Inc. (BX) gained 4.1% after S&P Dow Jones Indices said that the private equity firm will join the S&P 500 index.

The author, Kristen Jacks, worked *at Kiplinger's Personal Finance Magazine* where she learned the origins of various stock price moves

Clorox cyberattack reported on CNN

Chapter 4: Evaluating a Stock

Stock prices from Yahoo! Finance

P/E formula and definition from Investopedia.com

Dividends from Yahoo! Finance

John Bogle noted in his book, *Enough,* that dividends accounted for almost half of all stock investment gains from 1900 to 2007, page 53.

Chapter 5: What Is a Bond?

Real-world bond information from Fidelity Investments

The *Bond Buyer* reported that Bank of America, Goldman Sachs, and J.P. Morgan were among the top 10 bond underwriters in 1H23 – "In 1H23, underwriters see shake up in rankings" by Christina Baker on July 10, 2023

Bond features and definitions based on information from *Bonds: An Introduction to Core Concepts* by Mark Mobius c) 2012

Bond chapters reviewed by bond expert Sally Bednar

Chapter 6: Bond Prices

Real-world bond information from Fidelity Investments

Based on information from *Bonds: An Introduction to Core Concepts* by Mark Mobius c) 2012

Bond chapters reviewed by bond expert Sally Bednar

Chapter 7: Evaluating a Bond

Real-world bond information from Fidelity Investments

Bond ratings from S&P's Net Advantage and Fitch website

Based on information from *Bonds: An Introduction to Core Concepts* by Mark Mobius c) 2012

I bond information from Treasury Direct (www.treasurydirect.gov)

Bond chapters reviewed by bond expert Sally Bednar

Chapter 8: Mutual Funds

The author of this book, Kristen Jacks, worked for *Mutual Funds Magazine*. Content drawn from her extensive knowledge of mutual funds.

Chapter 9: Exchange-traded funds

Content drawn from the *Bogleheads on Investing* podcast, episode 15, and from YouTube videos with Eric Balchunas, the senior ETF analyst at Bloomberg.

Chapter 10: Cryptocurrency

Bitcoin prices from Yahoo! Finance

Content drawn from numerous early episodes of *Unchained*, the cryptocurrency podcast hosted by Laura Shin. Her interviews with Olaf Carlson-Wee were particularly helpful

Comments on Solana from Bloomberg Daybreak Weekend podcast on December 23, 2023. Tom Busby interviewed Mike McGlone, Bloomberg's senior commodity strategist, and Bloomberg Markets editor Michael Regan. Worth a listen if you are interested in the future of crypto.

Chapter 11: How to Buy Investments

True story about author's babysitter's husband

The author, Kristen Jacks, worked at *Kiplinger's Personal Finance Magazine* where she learned about brokers

Special thanks to Emma Goodness for her research on brokers

"Is your money safe?" pulls from various agency websites (SEC.gov, FDIC. gov, sipc.org, finra.org).

Chapter 12: The tax consequences of investing

The tax foundation estimates the U.S. tax code is "well over 1 million words."

I Bond tax treatment from Treasury Direct website (www.treasurydirect.gov)

Tax rules from various Internal Revenue Service (IRS) publications, including Pub. 550.

Tax section reviewed by tax expert Sunny Taylor

Chapter 13: Strategy Part I

Tiffany Aliche quote from *Get Good with Money*, p.170-71.

Quote from *The Latte Factor* by David Bach c) 2019, p. 82

Bankrate.com savings calculator

Chapter 14: Strategy Part I

History lesson drawn from numerous *Masters in Business* podcasts with passive investing diehards like John Bogle, Burton Malkiel, and Charles Ellis

28% of Vanguard S&P 500 Fund is seven stocks pulled from Vanguard website

Bond benchmarks
https://www.wsj.com/market-data/bonds/benchmarks

About the Author

Kristen Jacks is a financial educator and the Founder of Money in Your Twenties℠. Kristen studied financial planning at Boston University's Center for Professional Education. She started her career at *Kiplinger's Personal Finance Magazine* and later worked at *Mutual Funds Magazine*. Kristen is a graduate of Duke University.